to Bob

I give you this book
just as I plighted you my troth,
this is all that I am,
and I love you

TAMING YOUR INNER SUPERVISOR

BOOK ONE

by Ruth Haag

illustrated by Bob Haag

h·a·a·g

environmental

press

TAMING YOUR INNER SUPERVISOR   BOOK ONE

Text and Illustration Copyright © 1998 by Ruth S. Haag

Published by haag environmental press

Printed in the United States of America
For information contact: Haag Environmental Press, 1064 N. Main St #401, Bowling Green, OH 43402-1346

Library of Congress Catalog Card Number: 98-93328

ISBN 0-9665497-0-8

TABLE OF CONTENTS

CHAPTER 1...."CONGRATULATIONS! TODAY YOU ARE A SUPERVISOR"

A Story

Ruth woke up, excited to start her day. Today she was in charge of the Planetarium and its associated staff. She was pleased to be a supervisor, even if her official job title was "receptionist". She was 23 years old, she had graduated from college nearly 2 years ago. The "management" had obviously recognized her supervisory potential, her parents professed to be proud of her. She walked into her receptionist office and began to plan her first meeting with her staff. All seven of her planetarium demonstrator staff members came to her meeting. She gave no thought to the fact that until yesterday these seven people had reported to another person, and that person was still part of the group. She said:

> "We will continue to work as before. We will be changing a few things, but I will not make any changes unless we have all talked about it and all of us have agreed to it. Now, there is a problem with shows starting late and ending late. That messes up the schedule for museum tours (here she felt she was communicating extremely well), so you will need to start your shows on time."

She then adjourned her first staff meeting knowing that these people were hers, and that from this point forward only quality would come out of her "organization".

In the weeks which followed, the shows continued to start late. A planetarium demonstrator would generally arrive on time, go into the planetarium, and then just not open the doors of the room until the group of students had been waiting an average of five minutes. Two of the demonstrators continually arrived for work late. The air-conditioner broke and the room became something close to a tropical rain forest. Worse yet, Ruth started to listen to the shows given by her demonstrators, and one of them told an elementary school group that the moon was hollow! She caught one of her demonstrators arriving late, smiled at him, and said:

"You have to start coming on time".

She then smiled and walked off. "That was hard to do.", she thought, "but I had to". The demonstrator continued to come to work late.

First Thesis: No One is Prepared to be a Supervisor

Becoming a supervisor is often a very exciting proposition. The position of "supervisor"" is thought of in the business world as something to strive for, and is a social status-symbol once you attain it. It is fun at parties to say, "I am a supervisor of 3 people", or "my staff does...". Unfortunately, that is about where the fun ends. Supervising requires you to care about and be involved with other people, their successes, and their failures. It involves both understanding yourself and understanding your employees, and for many of us, those are not things which we really want to do.

Most often, new supervisors are chosen because they have been at the company for a specific amount of time, because they have the correct schooling related to what the company does, or because they are popular with the upper management.   It is rare that a new supervisor is chosen because they exhibit management skills. In Ruth's case, she was given the job because she was the only full-time staff member who knew astronomy.   Her "promotion" had absolutely nothing to do with her ability to supervise. Like most new supervisors, she was given no training for her new position.

Ruth's planetarium staff came late and gave bad shows not because they were bad people, or bad employees, but rather because Ruth was a bad (or she would prefer that you say) inexperienced supervisor. The employees were merely responding to the atmosphere which Ruth created. When Ruth reprimanded her tardy employees with a smile, they interpreted that she did not really mean it. They proved this when they continued to come late and Ruth did not say anything more. The atmosphere which Ruth had created was one where employees did come to work, but not one in which they felt obligated to come on time, or to do really good work.

Ninety percent of the time, "bad employees" or "ineffective workers" are a result of the atmosphere which the supervisor creates.

The task at hand is not to improve or motivate the employees, but rather to improve the supervisor.   In Ruth's case, she had to   learn to lead her staff in the direction which she wanted to go, in an atmosphere where she felt comfortable.

CHAPTER 2...THE FIRST MISTAKES OF A NEW SUPERVISOR

A Story About All Supervisor's First Mistakes and Problems

Ruth thought over her role as a supervisor that first evening. She was pretty confident that she would be a good supervisor. She wanted to be the type of supervisor whom employees looked up to. One who always gave good directions, one who even would help as a confidant if the employee would need it. She knew that she did not much like any of the supervisors to whom she had reported thus far in her own career. She was sure that she would not make the unreasonable decisions, as they had. She was sure that it would be easy to get her staff to like her, and that one way to accomplish this would be to only make decisions that the entire staff agreed upon.

Second Thesis: Everyone Makes the Same First Mistakes

The first day, a supervisor often has great expectations. Each new supervisor has had several years as an employee and has formed an opinion of what their supervisors should have done in many situations. Generally, each person feels that the job will be easy, and that they, themselves, will be better than all supervisors who have gone before them.

There are two main ideas that new supervisors seem to routinely come up with:

- all of the members of my staff will like me
- my group will be run as a democracy

The typical first goal of the new supervisor is to be well-liked by their staff. Everyone wants to be liked and accepted and feels that, even though they did not always like their previous (and even current) supervisors, that was some personality flaw in those people. They, on the other hand, will be congenial. They plan to give each staff member growth opportunities, and they plan to watch them work happily.

The typical second idea of the new supervisor is to run the group as a democracy. This ties in with the first goal. If the majority of the group agrees to the procedures, then they will all like the supervisor.

Ruth told the seven university students who were her first employees that she would not ever implement a change unless they had all agreed to it. In that case, she wasn't even worrying about a democracy, she planned to have unanimous approval of all of her ideas. She could not imagine a situation where they would not like one of her ideas.

More of The First Mistakes Story

Ruth discovered in the days which followed that various members of her staff seemed to have problems with her actions. One of the staff complained that she held her weekly meetings too early in the day. He arrived with red-rimmed eyes. Some of her staff seemed to actually feel that they knew more than she did about operating the planetarium, and disagreed with directions which she gave. Some members were irritated when she suggested that they wear a uniform for the weekend shows which were given to the general public. All were angry when she insisted that shows still be given even though the air-conditioner was broken. Often, she could not get them to agree with her, or with one another, on anything. It was a surprise to her that the person whose position she was now in did not seem to support what she was doing.

More of the Second Thesis...About Being Liked

The new supervisor soon discovers that some people in the group do not like them. Maybe they do not like the decisions the supervisor is making; maybe they do not like that the supervisor has had to reprimand them; maybe they do not like that they, themselves, were not given the supervisor position.

Everyone cannot like everyone else all of the time. In school, we accepted that some entire groups of students did not like us. The same is true in the business world. The new supervisor just has to come to an acceptance of this, and remember that there is a big difference between liking a person and respecting a person. The supervisor must always maintain the respect of their staff, but they do not have to be, and will never be, liked by everyone on their staff.

While running your group like a democracy sounds laudable, it is not, if you consider how difficult it is for the United States government to run as a democracy. Only half of the citizens of the United States vote at any one election. The losers in every decision spend years complaining about the loss, and continually want to vote on the issue again. It takes a long time to make any changes or progress with our government. Also, our country continually has a group of people suggesting that we should impeach the president. Obviously, you will not get much work done from your group if you run it like a democracy.

A Group is Helpless Without a Leader

Someone has to be responsible for the products of the group, and that someone is the supervisor. Someone has to make the decisions, especially if they are unpopular decisions (like to make everyone work late), and that someone is the supervisor. In businesses which have people working in dangerous situations, someone has to be responsible for the health and safety of the group, and that someone is the supervisor. The day-to-day decisions that a supervisor is responsible for are not decisions which can get made by a group voting. The groups cannot, for instance, vote on whether to use breathing air while cleaning hazardous wastes out of a confined space; the supervisor must decide. A group cannot vote on staying and working late; they will end up split and hostile toward the half of the group who "wins" the vote.

Summary of First Mistakes and Problems

Being a supervisor means that you will need to make decisions, and sometimes, those decisions will make people unhappy. A supervisor should always be respected, but may not always be liked.

CHAPTER 3...."LOOK TO YOURSELF", IT'S YOU, NOT THEM

The atmosphere which you create for your group causes the group to behave in a particular way.

If you were a perfect leader, your group would come to work on time each day, work hard and efficiently, take reasonable breaks, enjoy laughing and talking with their co-workers, and then leave a little later than expected.

If you are not a perfect leader, you group may come to work late, take long breaks, work for hours on the wrong project, have long gossip sessions with their peers, get done with their work and wait for you to assign new tasks, and then leave for home early.

Underneath it all, most of your "bad" employees are capable of doing good work, but they are actually being stopped from good performance or encouraged into bad performance because of the atmosphere which you have created.

A Story About the Three Little Supervisors

Three supervisors are standing in a parking lot watching an employee back a large truck. It becomes apparent that the employee is going to back the truck into the building. The first supervisor stands and watches. The second supervisor turns to the other two and asks:

"Do you think that they are going to back into the building? Should we do something about it?"

The third supervisor begins to yell at the employee to stop. The employee stops backing, just in time, and the building is not hit. The first supervisor starts to walk away, while watching the others. The second supervisor walks after the first supervisor and says:

"I think that we should have a training meeting on safety while moving equipment around here. Henry never trains his people thoroughly enough."

The third supervisor walks up to the truck and begins yelling at the driver:

"What did you think you were doing? It is company policy to not back a vehicle without a spotter. You were told that when you started to work here!"

The supervisors start to walk to the building. The first supervisor stays back some and, when the others are out of hearing range, says to the truck driver:

"Eric is having a stressful day, he didn't know that you were trying hard. Keep up the good work."

The same three supervisors are now preparing to walk into the building. The first supervisor meekly goes through the door, looking at the floor. The second supervisor asks:

"Do you think that they are ready for us yet? Should we go in or wait outside?"

The third supervisor boldly walks in, looking at all of the workers and begins to yell:

"Don't all of you people know that you are supposed to have hard-hats on? I want you to all stop working this instant, and find your hard-hats!"

Third Thesis: There are Three Supervisor "Personalities"

Everyone views the world and their place in it, in a slightly different way. Some seem very humble, some seem overly confident and some seem angry at much of the world, much of the time. When a person becomes a supervisor it is this view that they have of themselves and their place in the world which influences their initial actions. The supervisor's actions, in turn, cause their group to behave in certain ways. When a supervisor is too humble, for instance, they might not be able to respond quickly enough to a problem. Knowing this, their employees will more frequently disobey orders. When a supervisor is too angry at the world, they yell at their employees too much. Knowing this their employees will ignore them. When a supervisor is too worried about losing their job, they control their employees too much. Knowing this, their employees rebel, and refuse to do any work.

A supervisor is a leader who ideally needs to be firm, responsible, knowledgeable, decisive, and fair. This is very difficult to do if you happen to feel that the rest of the people in the world are better than you are, or if you are afraid that you will lose your job, or if you are angry much of the time. In order to become a really good supervisor, you will need to first be able to acknowledge what you are like, and then learn to tame those parts of your personality which conflict with your ability to supervise.

CHAPTER 4...THE SENSITIVE SUPERVISOR

A Story About a Sensitive Supervisor

Remember Ruth's smiling reprimand of her employee who came to work late? Her employee came to work late for the next six months. He got to do this until Ruth returned from an "Assertive Supervisor" seminar.

Sensitive Supervisor Defined

Ruth is a sensitive supervisor. Sensitive supervisors are afraid to actually tell someone what they are thinking. When they assign work, they tend to apologize and offer to do some of the task themselves. They fear that the employee will have their feelings hurt (and then not like the supervisor), or that the employee may say something rude in response to the assignment. The sensitive supervisor simply does not want to confront anyone. In the "Three Little Supervisor" story, the sensitive supervisor is the one who will wait and watch a truck back into a building, will try to "smooth things out" with the reprimanded employee, and will enter a room looking at the floor.

Many people do not want to admit that they are sensitive. If they are in a supervisor meeting and it is suggested that they have a talk with their employee, they will immediately agree to have the talk. A month later, when they are asked how the talk went, they will say "I didn't do it yet." Their reasons are varied, but predictable:

"I couldn't get the person alone."

"They didn't seem so bad this month."

"Their (family member) was sick and I didn't want to upset them."

"I thought I'd wait to see if they improved on their own."

The sensitive supervisor often knows clearly what needs to be done to lead the group, but has a very difficult time bringing themselves to do it.

The Employee's Response to the Sensitive Supervisor

Employees of sensitive supervisors tend to "get away" with bad activities. They come to work a little late, and leave a little early. They may be asked to correct a product and will generally just not do it. They ask for and receive more time off, longer lunch hours, and more sick days, because their sensitive supervisor does not want to hurt their feelings by making them work. You can find the sensitive supervisor working late into the night, finishing up projects that the staff was supposed to do, while their entire staff is at home watching a TV special. In extreme cases, the sensitive supervisor actually begins to receive and perform assignments given to them by their employees. The end result for a sensitive supervisor is that they are walked upon by their employees. They are liked, but not necessarily respected, by their employees.

CHAPTER 5...THE BELLIGERENT SUPERVISOR

A Story About a Belligerent Supervisor

Paul walked into the shop and began to yell. A wrench was laying on the counter and not in the appropriate tool box. The garbage can was full to over-flowing. He yelled at the room in general. The three people in the room continued to do their work with their heads bent down. A person who was on a tour associated with their interview became visibly uneasy. The wrench was left where it was.

Belligerent Supervisor Defined

Paul is an example of a belligerent supervisor. Belligerent supervisors are people who were brought up with the "boot camp approach" and thrived upon it. They can take the challenge of hearing, "Your work stinks", and come back fighting. Often, they excelled at sports in their former life. They can be paired with other belligerent people, have violent arguments, apologize, shake hands, and start all over again. Most of the work that they assign is "urgent". Belligerent supervisors tend to yell first and ask questions later. They often have high blood pressure. In "The Three Little Supervisors" story, they were represented by the supervisor who was willing to yell at the employee who was backing into the building, and also the one who entered the room and immediately reprimanded the people who were there.

The Employee's Response to a Belligerent Supervisor

Employees of belligerent supervisors tend to be quiet. They make sure that they arrive and leave at the same time as their supervisor. They are often overworked, because they do not have the courage to tell their supervisor that they already had a task, when a new one is handed to them. They often feel that their supervisor is arbitrary, because it seems that they are working on one task and are suddenly moved to another of lesser importance, then yelled at because they did not get the first task done. These employees are very frustrated much of the time. They also become immune to the yelling, and begin to ignore it. This, of course, makes the belligerent supervisor yell more. The employees generally fear, rather than like or respect, the belligerent supervisor.

CHAPTER 6...THE REGAL SUPERVISOR

A Story About a Regal Supervisor

Henry had been a supervisor of scientists for three months. Many had come and gone in his position. He was so proud of his corner office but, deep down, he was worried that he might do something to lose it. He was also worried that his staff would do something to make him look bad. He tried to watch their every move so that this would not happen.

Henry had to work on annual employee evaluations. He was worried that he might do a bad job on the evaluations. He decided that he had to concentrate on them. The best way to concentrate would be to have no distractions. He decided to lock his office door to keep his employees out. He rationalized that the evaluations were very important, he had to do a good job, and he certainly did not want employees seeing each other's evaluations on his desk.

While Henry was thus closeted, one of his scientists had to ask him a question about an overdue report, before it could be finished. He went to Henry's office and found the door locked. Incredulous, he rattled the door knob. Henry's secretary came to the door and explained that Henry had important work to do for the next two days, and could not answer any questions. The already overdue report had to wait for two more days, for Henry to be free.

Regal Supervisor Defined

Henry is a regal supervisor. Regal supervisors are nearly consumed with fear of making a mistake and being fired. In "The Three Little Supervisors" story, Henry would be the supervisor who would ask the others if maybe they should intercede and he would ask the others if it would be all right to enter the building. He only wants to make a decision if he is first sure that others agree with him.

The fear of making a mistake, or of an employee making a mistake and causing the regal supervisor to be fired, consumes their thoughts. In order to make sure that they do not make a mistake, regal supervisors try to control nearly every move of their employees. They give out assignments in little bites, so that the employee will have to check back often. The regal supervisor tries to make sure that they appear "supervisory" at all times. They tend to order subordinates to bring them coffee, papers, and pencils. They allow themselves to be interrupted when they are in meetings, and tend to be too busy to get to appointments with subordinates on time.

The regal supervisor tries to keep things confused at all times. That way, if something does go wrong, it is difficult to determine if they were to blame or not. They are willing to blame their subordinates for a mistake, in order to save themselves.

The Employee Response to a Regal Supervisor

Employees of regal supervisors are often found waiting for their supervisor to be free to assign their next task, or to make a decision on the current task. Their employees use their prodigious amounts of free time gossiping about what is going on with their supervisor, the company, and other members of the staff. The employees have no real allegiance to the supervisor since they are made to wait for long periods of time for instructions, and at times are blamed if something does go wrong. Eventually, the employees either refuse to work for the supervisor, or they openly challenge the supervisor and step around them in the chain of command.

CHAPTER 7...BEGINNING THE TAMING OF THE THREE SUPERVISORS

The Taming

Since your personality has created an atmosphere where your employees are either too free, too frightened, or too confused and alone, you are going to have to tame your personality and create a new atmosphere. You are going to have to make a change in how you think about your employees, and how you talk to them.

Taming of the Sensitive Supervisor

For the sensitive supervisor, the time when employee-supervisor interactions most often go astray, is during the time that the supervisor is telling the employee that they are displeased with some aspect of the employee's performance.

The first thing that the sensitive supervisor has to accept is that they are going to have to tell people things which they do not want to hear. They are going to have to hurt other people's feelings.

A Story About a Confrontation

Cindy knew that she would have to confront Alex about his coming to work late. Her stomach had been in knots for days, preparing for her talk with Alex. Alex arrived in her office and she began:

"Alex, you consistently arrive to work late. This disrupts everyone else's schedule, and it will have to stop."

While she spoke, her voice quavered and she looked at her hands in her lap. She hoped that Alex did not know that she was nervous. Alex said:

"I get to work late because the traffic is so bad, I can't help it."

Cindy replied:

"Then you need to start earlier each day."

Alex said:

"You never required me to come to work on time before. You are angry with me for some other reason."

Cindy replied, still looking at her hands:

"No, I just want you to get to work on time".

To this Alex said:

"You must be having a problem with your toddler at home. I don't envy you, working full-time and having a toddler at home."

Finally, Cindy looked straight at Alex and said:

"We are not talking about me, we are talking about you, and you have to come to work on time, starting tomorrow. This discussion is over."

Cindy rose from her chair and escorted Alex out of the room.

An Analysis of the Confrontation

The sensitive supervisor has to come to accept that a face-to-face talk with the employee <u>will</u> have to happen. Plan a brief talk where you state your feelings about what has happened, and what you are going to require for it to be fixed. Since your nature is to not want to do this, you will be inclined to want to make the talk last a long time, and remove some of the "punch" from it. Keep it short and sweet. A talk like this should last no longer than five minutes. A talk as short as one minute is OK, and anything lasting longer than a half of an hour is so long that there will have been no point in doing the talk at all.

You must talk to the person as near to the time of the problem as possible. You cannot wait until two months later and try to reform a problem. You also cannot have someone else do the talking for you.

DO NOT apologize for having to reprimand the employee. If you say:

"I am not pleased with your behavior."

It will mean much more than:

"I'm really sorry, but you may have made a mistake."

Likewise, nervous giggling really ruins the talk. With a straight face say:

"This report is not done according to the standards which we set."

As opposed to:

(giggle, chuckle) "This is not too good."

Do not beg:

"Please do better."

Or mumble:

"Mm, I think, mm you mmcould do better."

Do not try to form the apology for the employee:

"You probably were coming down with the flu and that is why this is bad."

Keep the blame on the employee, do not accept part of it . Saying:

"I probably was not clear."

Will give the employee the opening to decide that the problem was caused by you. Rather say:

"You did not do this correctly."

You will need to look as close to the person's eyes as you comfortably can. Their nose or forehead is OK, the ground or corner of the room is not. They will notice if you are not confident and will use this to dismiss your talk.

Be sure of your facts before you start the talk. Do not allow the employee to verbally fight with you. The person may want to engage in an analysis of why you have misinterpreted the situation; refuse to listen to this. Remember that your talk is to be brief, have an ending statement, like:

"I expect to see the corrected document on my desk by 5 PM today".

And then leave. If you are in your office, stand up and escort the person to the door.

The Employee's Response to a Newly Reformed Sensitive Supervisor

Do not fool yourself into thinking that the employee has not noticed that you are sensitive. They will generally try to use this to their advantage during their first experience of you confronting them. They will attempt to drift the talk back to you in order to make you feel bad.

They will use a series of predictable phrases:

"You must be having a bad day."

"You are still feeling sick aren't you?"

"Is your child doing better?"

"Are you sure that you are allowed to discipline me?"

"Your job must be pretty hard, I don't envy you."

All of these ploys try to show you that they are not the problem, it is your personal situation which is the problem. Keep the conversation focused on them, not you.

You created the environment which has encouraged the beast which your employee has become. If you keep in control of the situation from now on, they will become good, respectful employees.

A Word About Hiring and Firing by Sensitive Supervisors

The sensitive supervisor feels real compassion for a person being interviewed. They are most inclined to "give the person a chance", and they will hire most people unless they have a partner to "bounce the facts off of". If they can talk over their findings from the interview with someone, they can easily get the courage to decide not to hire an unlikely candidate.

On the other hand, sensitive supervisors have no real difficulty firing an employee. When the employee has misbehaved badly, the sensitive supervisor begins to feel angry and betrayed. They might think something like:

"I worked so hard, and was so nice to this person, and they still stole money from the company."

They can march up to the person with confidence and firmly say:

"You are fired."

What the Sensitive Supervisor Will Not Be Able to Tame

It is nearly impossible for a sensitive supervisor to do an "instant reprimand". It is so against their nature to confront another person, that even when faced with a major transgression by an employee, they will have to think about it a little. The goal, then, is to be able to confront the employee as soon as possible after the problem occurs.

Taming of the Belligerent Supervisor

The belligerent supervisor wants to complain about every little problem as soon as they see it. They get themselves into trouble because they often have not taken enough time to analyze the situation. They make a wrong judgment, and yell at the wrong person for the wrong reason.

A Story About the Wrong Way

Kathy walked into the office and saw that the telephone was ringing, and Ed was talking to Rob intensely in the corner. She yelled:

"Ed, why aren't you answering the phone?"

Ed blanched and ran to answer it. He spoke into it and then waited and hung up. Kathy asked in an irritated tone:

"Why didn't you talk to the people?

Ed meekly responded:

"A fax machine has gotten our voice number. We have already had three calls in the last five minutes. Rob and I were just wondering if we tried not answering the next call if that would stop it."

An Analysis of the Mistake

The belligerent person often accuses the first person that they see, and most of the time is angry when they do it. About half of the time that a belligerent person wants to reprimand an employee, there is no need to. Either the belligerent supervisor has not understood what happened, or understands the problem, but has not found the correct culprit. At times, the belligerent supervisor has actually caused the problem by giving instructions poorly.

Never reprimand in anger. If you are red-faced-angry, walk away and calm down. You may even have to wait until the next day.

After you are calm, think over what happened that you were displeased with.

- What did you ask your employee to do?

- What is on their task list?

- Are they capable of doing what you assigned?

- When did you assign the task?

- Has there been any chance for the employee to work on the task between the time of assignment and now?

- Are you sure that the task is not actually done?

Your method of talking to the person must change from one of accusations, to one of looking for insight. Remember that most of the time, the person will have done something wrong because of mis-communication. They probably already know that it is wrong, but they are afraid to tell you. They know that you will yell at them. Give them a chance to talk first.

A Story About a Discussion

Joe saw Alice working on the report which was supposed to have been sent to the client the day before. He had a flash of anger thinking, "Why didn't it get done on time?" "These people are incompetent!" He took a deep breath, and said to Alice, in as pleasant a tone as he could muster,

"What sorts of problems did you have that prevented you from finishing the report on time?"

He waited patiently for Alice to answer. Finally she said:

"Remember, the client called two days ago and said that she did not want the report sent for another week, because she would be out of town?, Then Henry asked me to finish up work on another project.

Now I am back on this report, and expect to have it ready by the end of today."

Joe smiled, and walked back into his office.

A New Rule to Live By...Always Ask

The inclination of the belligerent supervisor is to yell first and listen later. However, they need to ask questions in a non-threatening manner, and listen to the responses. Once again, if you are red-faced angry, walk away and wait until you are calm.

Asking questions such as:

"What sorts of problems did you have?"

Or making statements such as:

"I was upset when I saw that the report was not done on time."

Will allow the person to explain what happened, rather than throw them into defensive mode as would happen if you said:

"I can't believe that you are so dumb."

Or :

"A person with your education should not have done this."

Or even:

"WHY ISN'T THIS REPORT DONE?"

If, after you have calmly asked, you discover that the person was indeed "bad", then tell them briefly what actions you are unhappy with, and what will be needed to fix the problem. Try saying:

"The deadline was yesterday, you should have informed me that you were going to miss it. I think that you will be able to get it done today by 5 PM. Please call me at noon and update me as to your status."

The Employee's Response to a Newly Tamed Belligerent Supervisor

If you have been yelling at your staff for a good number of months, this will be a dramatic change for them. They will actually begin to listen to you for the first time in a long while. They will most likely respond positively, and with some relief.

A Word About Hiring and Firing by Belligerent Supervisors

Early in their career, the belligerent supervisor will hire anyone who they interview, and figure that everyone will find a niche somewhere in the company. As the years go on, and they discover that some people are "nicheless", they change over to not wanting to hire anyone who they interview.

When it comes to firing, a most surprising thing happens: They cannot do it.

What the Belligerent Supervisor Will Not Be Able to Tame

Oddly enough, the belligerent supervisor finds it nearly impossible to fire someone. While they can suspend a person on a moment's notice, they cannot bring themselves to do the actual firing. This of course, only presents a problem if an employee needs to be fired. In one company this problem was solved by referring all "firing situations" to a person of a higher level, who was a sensitive supervisor. All affected supervisors participated in meetings to decide what to do, but it was up to the sensitive supervisor to say those difficult words "You are fired".

Taming of the Regal Supervisor

The regal supervisor faces each decision with these thoughts:

"What does my supervisor think?"

"What do my peers think?"

"Will I get promoted?"

"Will I lose my job?"

"Will I look important to others?"

Their decision-making thoughts need to become:

"What is right for my employee?"

"Will this help them to grow as people?"

"Have I given them as much responsibility as I can?"

"What is right for the project?"

"What is right for the company?"

The employee-supervisor interactions which cause regal supervisors the most trouble are those dealing with work assignments and staff meetings.

A Story About a Meeting

James had a weekly meeting with his staff. Since not all of the staff members had arrived yet, James had an inclination to use the extra time to call a client. Then he remembered that he should focus on his staff. He instead went into the meeting room, listened to his staff talking to one another, and then started the meeting on time. James remembered that he was supposed to share as much information with his staff as possible, so he began,

"I have an appointment tomorrow and will not be available to you for much of the day."

He looked at his staff and saw that they looked confused. He was generally available and they could not understand why he would be unavailable. He then added,

"I am going to be off tomorrow in order to be a chaperone at my kindergartner's field trip. I want to make sure that you all know what your assignmemts are, and give you a chance to ask questions of me now."

James was inclined to tell each staff member just one more assignment, so that each of them would have to check back with him later in the day, but he looked back at his notes, and instead said:

> "As a group, we need to produce the data tables for the report which is due on Friday. Sally, do you think you will be able to do the set-up on the computer?, Ed, can you and Charlie work on the data? Does anyone have any ideas as to how we can get it delivered to the client on Saturday?"

James noticed that he had forgotten to bring in his cup of coffee, so he said:

> "Sally, go and get my coffee from my desk."

Sally looked irritated, but she got up and then James remembered that he was not supposed to ask for "perks" from his staff. He called after Sally:

> "Wait a minute, why don't I go and get coffee for both of us."

Sally smiled at this and agreed.

Give Out Responsibility and Information

As a regal supervisor, you have to school yourself to give out as much information and responsibility as is necessary. You have to replace your worry about your own performance with a dedication to enabling your employees to work, and work successfully.

No Perks

You will need to be careful about asking for extra "perks" from your employees. Make sure that you get your own coffee and sharpen your own pencils. Up to now, you have been using your employees to enhance your image as a supervisor, and they do not like it.

The Employee's Response to a Newly Tamed Regal Supervisor

When you start to concentrate on your employees, including giving more responsibility to them, you will notice that more work gets done. You will also notice that, as you ask for fewer "perks", your employees will support you more and agree to do extra work without grumbling.

A Word About Hiring and Firing by Regal Supervisors

The regal supervisor sees all new employees as a possible threat to their position. Therefore, they do not like anyone who they interview and want to reject them all.

The regal supervisor has no problem firing people; it is a relief to get rid of the threat.

What the Regal Supervisor Will Not Be Able to Tame

Regal supervisors find it nearly impossible to handle a direct challenge from an employee. If the employee stands up and says "I refuse to do the work", you most likely will be unable to respond.   In such an instance, it would help if you had a pre-planned response. One idea would be to say "You are directly questioning my authority, you should go and take a break and come back in 15 minutes and we will talk." That will buy you some time to figure out what to do, and not compromise your authority.

A Summary

The sensitive supervisor wants to avoid employee problems and hopes that they will go away. The belligerent supervisor wants to complain about every little problem as soon as they see it. The regal supervisor is so concerned about losing their own job that they want to keep control of every move their employees make.

The sensitive supervisor's employees begin to assign work to them. The belligerent supervisor's employees ignore them. The regal supervisor's employees eventually rebel and refuse to work.

The sensitive supervisor needs to confront people. The belligerent supervisor needs to stop and think. The regal supervisor needs to give out information and responsibility.

All of this advice is joined by a common thread:

Think about your people, do not think about yourself.

CHAPTER 8... "IS THIS WORKING?" EVALUATING YOUR SUPERVISING

A Story about Monday Mornings

Every Monday at Haag Environmental Company started slowly. The field crews could not seem to get their equipment loaded into their vans and leave. The field supervisors did not seem to know what they were supposed to do that week. The person in charge of the office felt rushed and pushed around and became unhappy. The person in charge of cost/schedule control would then burst into angry yelling and table pounding. During most of this time, the field technicians were enjoying themselves by talking to one another while they were waiting for their supervisors to come to give them their assignments. Then, the senior staff would go into the meeting room, close the doors and not come out for an hour and a half. When they did come out, more frustration would occur, because the crews would not have left yet. The crews would typically leave at 3:00 PM on Monday, not 10:00 AM as planned.

The supervisors decided to set out to solve these problems. The supervisors found two "how to supervise" books. The first book provided great volumes of information about "standard problem employee types" and how to deal with them. This was pretty neat. It showed the problem-employee types, and recommended what to say to fix their performance problems. There were nice pictures of animals by the different types of problems. Each supervisor started to read the book, got a little bogged down, but resolved to consult it when the next problem arose. The Supervisors found it difficult to consult the book while the employee was talking to them. The book was lost. There was some discussion of looking for it, but not one ever did.

The second "how to supervise" book which one of the supervisors got provided easy "standard program types". These involved things like self esteem programs, employee reward programs, and programs which suggested that the supervisor move around more to observe what was happening. One of the supervisors suggested that the Monday morning problems would be solved if a reward system was instituted. They suggested stock options and T-shirts. Some supervisors began to look at T-shirt catalogs, and calculate the price of the proposed reward program. After several weeks they were ready to start their program. They announced to the field technicians that the first crew to be ready to leave for the field would receive the new T-shirts.

The first week, a crew was ready to leave at 2:30 PM. That was somewhat later than the hoped-for 10 AM, but was earlier than the usual 3:00 PM, so the supervisors awarded the T-shirts. The second week, a different crew was ready to leave at 1:00 PM. They got the T-shirts. The next week the same crew was ready by 12:30 PM. The supervisors decided that T-shirts as a repeat to a crew would be useless. The third crew, which did not have T-shirts, started to get ready later and later. At 4:00 PM on that Monday they were asked what their problem was. The replied that since they would never be faster than the other two crews, they had simply stopped trying. They suggested that they just wait and leave Tuesday morning.

One supervisor was in the shop while the crews were loading their vehicles. They heard the crew members laughing about the T-shirts:

"Do they really expect us to like those things?"

"Who would ever wear fushia? "

"My spouse is using it as a rag."

The First Question: "What are we trying to do?"

Whenever there is a problem with things getting accomplished, you need to ask yourself "What are we trying to do?" You have to keep focused on the end goal in order to see through the confusion caused by the problem.

In the case of the Monday Mobilization, Haag Environmental Company was trying to get field crews on the road traveling to work sites by 10:00 AM each Monday.

The Second Question: "Is This Working?"

Once you have decided what you are really trying to do, you need to ask "Is it working?" This is a hard question to answer honestly, unless you step away from the problem. Often a supervisor is emotionally involved in all of the confusion, and is angry about the outcome, and thus cannot make an honest evaluation. The supervisors at Haag Environmental Company were probably too upset at the staff for not liking the T-shirts to be able to do an honest evaluation. Suffice it to say, if you are not accomplishing what you are setting out to do, it is not working.

If Haag Environmental Company was trying to get on their way to the field on time, their T-shirt reward approach was clearly <u>not</u> working.

Even if they tried out other methods proposed by the books which they were using, they would again see that the "motivate the employee" or "talk firmly to the employee" approaches would not solve the problem. They stopped just short of trying a "team building" exercise.

A Story About a Success

The supervisors at Haag Environmental Company faced up to the fact that they were trying to get their crews mobilized and it was not working.

They looked carefully at themselves and found that they had too many other activities conflicting with the time needed to prepare field crews to leave for work sites. To reduce confusion and conflicts, they did the following:

- The senior staff meeting was moved to a time other than Monday morning, making these people available to help.

- The field supervisors started to meet before Monday morning to do their planning for the next week.

- Extra staff members, who were not needed to complete the mobilization process, were asked to come in late on Monday mornings, thereby lessening the congestion.

After this, the crews were out the door by 10:00 A.M. each Monday!

A Final Note About This Story

It is important to notice that the problems with Monday mornings at Haag Environmental Company were not caused by the field crews being lazy people. The problem was caused by the atmosphere created by the senior staff. Once the atmosphere was changed, the field crews worked very hard.

Learning how to "talk effectively" to the field crews, or giving them rewards, would not help if they did not know what they were supposed to be loading and into which vehicles. Once they found out what they were supposed to be doing, they happily did it.

How to Identify If Something Is Not Working

A program or system of management is not working if:

- The goal of the program is never accomplished.

- The staff is irritated with one another (and you) during the project.

- The project is always done late "by the skin of your teeth".

If any of these things are happening, you need to carefully look over your system and find the problem areas. Most likely you will find:

- You have not planned the project well enough ahead of time.

- You are trying to get too many things accomplished at one time.

- Your people are not being used well; some are waiting for others to work before they can start.

- You have not allowed enough time to get the project done.

- Your people are assigned incorrectly; they cannot actually do the task which you have given them.

After you identify what is going wrong, all you have to do is change it.

A Story About a Late Tour

Ruth was greeting school groups who had arrived for their tour of the museum. The 60 elementary students arrived about fifteen minutes early. They met in the rotunda of the museum. The rotunda was made entirely of travertine (holey limestone) and the echoes were pretty neat. The only problem was that university classes were begin given on the second floor in the rotunda area, and the professors were quite annoyed at the noisy children. The group waited fifteen minutes, trying to contain their noise. Finally 10 o'clock arrived, and the teacher asked Ruth where the tour guides were. Ruth explained, as she had many times over the past year, that the tour guides were university students, and their classes ended on the hour. Given that it took about ten minutes to get from one place to the other on the campus, the guides would arrive very soon. The teacher asked then if the tour time would be extended to accommodate the late start. Ruth explained that the guides had classes to go to and therefore could not stay longer.

The guides finally arrived. Ruth hurried them into the building, told them to go hang up their coats and get to their groups. The guides walked to the coat room, chatting to one another. They seemed irritated when Ruth rushed in and said:

"You are late getting the tour started, you must hurry."

"I'll just run my tour late", one guide said.

Ruth angrily replied:

"No, all of the tours must end at the same time, hurry up!"

The tours finally started 15 minutes late. The school teachers were angry about the shortened time, the guides were irritated about being rushed, and the professors were really angry about the half hour of noise which they had just put up with.

What Was Going Wrong?

Something was wrong with this picture. The school groups were being required to arrive on the hour, and to leave on the hour, but their tour guides could not possibly arrive until quarter after the hour. The tour guides did not appreciate being rushed to start a tour as soon as they walked in the door. Also, school children were being asked to be quiet in the best echo chamber ever imagined.

A Story About the Solution

Ruth suggested to her supervisor that they schedule tours to begin and end at a quarter after the hour. This way, the university students would have time to arrive, take off their coats and get settled before they began their tours. Also, Ruth suggested that tour guides not be scheduled for a tour unless they had a two-hour time block open. That would allow the schedule to be able to shift somewhat.

Ruth also developed a set of worksheets for the students who arrived early. She scrounged up a box of pencils and crayons, and had staff members make up dot-to-dot pictures of major museum exhibits. Ruth included museum information on the back of the worksheets, so that, if they were taken home, the parents would know where the museum was, and how to get there.

Summary

The problem was not with the employees, or the clients, but rather was with the supervisor's set-up of the program. When a project or program repeatedly does not work, DO NOT ask yourself:

"What is wrong with my employees?"

"Why is everyone so dumb, except me?"

DO ask yourself:

"What are we trying to do?"

"Is it working?"

After you figure out the answers to these two questions, change the program.

CHAPTER 9...EMOTIONS AND SUPERVISING

A Story About Emotional Supervising

Eric looked at each day as a challenge to get through. It seemed to him that most events of the day were nearly impossible to overcome. His morning commute to work was just the start. Sometimes, he would arrive with his nerves nearly shot. Today, when he walked into the office, Ed met him and told him that the meeting to present their monthly figures had been moved up from noon to 10 a.m. Eric could not believe his bad luck. He decided to get a cup of coffee and discovered that the coffee maker was broken. Sam came into Eric's office and said:

"My son is ill. The doctor wants him to go to the hospital today for some tests, may I take a longer lunch hour so that I can be with him?"

Eric shouted:

"No, you can't have any extra time off! The meeting has been moved up, and we have to all work very hard to prepare!"

Sam left the office mystified. The meeting occurred on schedule and it was a great success. Eric was very happy. John came into his office and asked:

"May I take a longer lunch hour? I need to buy a new pair of shoes."

Eric replied:

"Of course, no problem."

Emotions and Supervising

A supervisor needs to have an ability to remove their emotions from their decisions. It is often helpful to remember Victorians when learning about this concept. During the Victorian era, it was improper to discuss personal problems or to show emotions. Ladies who were pregnant were closeted away after they began to "show". After the baby was born, no mention was made about where it may have come from. A proper Victorian adult did not show extremes of happiness or sorrow.

Although, these days, this may seem a little extreme for everyday life, this Victorian lack of emotion is proper for a supervisor when they are dealing with their employees. You need to make all of your employee decisions based on your goals and plans, and not based on your own current emotional situation.

About Eric's Story

In the story about Eric's emotional decision, you can see that his response to Sam was pretty irrational. The meeting which Eric was worried about would be over before the time that Sam needed to have off. Eric was so worried about his meeting that he was essentially saying to Sam:

"Can't you see I am too worried to answer any questions now?"

But, of course, that is not what Sam heard. Eric's response to John was just as emotional, but this time Eric was happy. Your employees need you to be in control of your emotions while you are making decisions about them.

CHAPTER 10...GOALS AND SUPERVISING

A Story About Too Many Decisions

Ruth was exhausted after her first two days as a supervisor. She had had no idea that her days would be consumed with decisions, like:

"Can I have next Wednesday off?"

"I am afraid to do a star show for high school students. Can't someone else do it?"

"Can four-year-olds come to the public planetarium shows?"

Part of what made it exhausting was that she did not know what her answer was to any of these questions. Over time, she discovered where she stood on each of these issues, and was able to answer the questions which had previously taken her some thought and agony, quickly and decisively. She was able to answer:

"Yes, you can have Wednesday off, but only if you notify me a week in advance."

"I will go over how to handle high school students with you and you can sit in on Joe's show to see how he does it before you do your show."

"Yes, all children can come to the public show, but it is 45 minutes long and they have to be quiet. Can your child do that?"

Finding answers became less difficult as she developed goals for her museum programs.

What is a Goal?

The concept of goals is still somewhat elusive to some people. They tend to decide that goals are for planners, not them. Also, some goals (especially those called mission statements) are so weighty that they cannot be understood by anyone.

Let us instead talk in plain English. Your goals should address:

- What do you want to accomplish?

- How do you want to accomplish it?

- Who are you going to accomplish it with?

you decide early on where you are going, how you are getting there, and with whom you are going, you will find that your day-to-day decisions will be much easier, and questioned less often by your employees.

For example, if your goal is to get work done in record time and your plan to get there is to work your employees long hours, then when your employee asks for personal time off, you will not grant it, because it will not help you to get work done in record time.

If, on the other hand, your goal is to produce a consistent, reliable product and your plan to do it is to have the same employees happily working for you for the next 20 years, you will most likely grant the time off, because you know that this will keep your employees happy and loyal, and they will get the work done when they return.

You will need to have both corporate goals which are consistent with those of your company, and personal goals for your employees' growth as people.

Examples of corporate goals are:

- Maximize profit

- Produce good products

- Produce products efficiently

Examples of goals which a supervisor might have for their employees are:

- Learn to do their job to the best of their ability

- Develop a feeling of satisfaction with their job

- Provide an opportunity to grow professionally

A Word About Ruth's Decisions

Ruth was finally able to make the decisions in the story because she had come up with a plan of where she and her organization were going.

As a corporate service goal, she had decided that she would serve the members of the public who came to her planetarium, and would provide for them the programs the way that they requested them. While these may seem like "crudely simple" goals, they were, in fact, a reversal of her predecessor's policies.

For her employee goals, she determined that her college-student employees would need to learn to be responsible about their jobs, and would be provided training for any new tasks which came up.

Having set these goals, she was able to make her decisions in the story, with ease.

Do Not Forget to Help Your Employees Grow

Supervisors become so focused on getting their own jobs done, that they often forget about the professional growth of their employees. As a supervisor, it is in your hands to see that your employees advance as much as they are able.

Each individual employee's direction will be a little different, however there are some overriding concepts:

- Your employees need to learn to do their own jobs, and do them well.

- Your employees need to learn to do new tasks as they are able.

- Your employees need to have the opportunity to advance, if they desire. (Sometimes, this advancement involves your employee leaving the company.)

A Story About a Brochure

Eleanor took her job because she could not find one in her area of expertise. Although she worked her hardest, she was not really happy. Her supervisor knew this. She knew that Eleanor was trained in marketing and writing. The company decided to re-make their brochure. Eleanor's supervisor suggested that the job be given to Eleanor.

Eleanor worked on the brochure, with her supervisor's oversight. The company was so pleased with the product, that they asked Eleanor to work on more marketing projects for them. Eleanor was promoted into the marketing department.

About Eleanor's Story

By helping Eleanor to find work that she liked, Eleanor's supervisor lost a good worker to another department. It was the right thing to do.

CHAPTER 11...ETHICS AND SUPERVISING

Ethics require you to draw the line between "right" and "wrong". Your supervisory ethics determine how far you are willing to go, to get some job done. A supervisor needs to decide where the line is, <u>before</u> the difficult decisions arrive.

A Story About a Mortgage Application

Carl was an average employee. He was working in a technician's position and that seemed to be the level of responsibility which he wanted to assume. He had been working at various technician jobs in various companies for the past six years. He was newly married and wanted to buy a house. He and his wife went to the bank to apply for a mortgage. The mortgage loan officer explained to Carl that he did not make enough money at his hourly wage to qualify for a loan for the house that he wanted to buy. The loan officer asked Carl if he often worked overtime. If that were the case, he explained, the overtime wages could be calculated into the total wage base, and perhaps then, Carl would qualify for the loan. Carl assured the mortgage loan officer that he did indeed often work overtime. He filled out the paperwork and happily left. Carl got home and immediately called his supervisor:

> "I'm applying for a mortgage. The bank is going to send you some information asking you to verify my employment."

His supervisor said:

"No problem, I fill out these forms all of the time, I'd be happy to do one for you"

Then, Carl revealed his plan:

"I told the mortgage loan officer that I work 10 hours a week of overtime. Can you just fill that into the places on the form? Otherwise, I won't be able to buy the house."

The Supervisor's Dilemma

The supervisor now has a bit of a problem. If he refuses to help Carl, Carl might resign, and he needs him to finish up a big project. On the other hand, if he lies on the mortgage information, Carl might then demand that he be given the 10 hours a week overtime which is now documented. Also all salary information is reported to so many government agencies that the correct data would be easily discoverable, as would the fact that the application information was falsified.

A Story About a "Helpful Lawyer"

Raj was an immigrant to the United States. He had a visa which allowed him to work and live in the United States, but not to remain indefinitely. He wanted to become a permanent citizen. The immigration laws stated that Raj would need to show that he was a type of worker that was in short supply in the United States, such as a medical worker, or that he had special one-of-a-kind skills, like a rock musician. Raj was a biologist with a bachelor's degree.

Raj hired an immigration attorney who charged him $1,000 to start work and promised to charge another $2,000 when the proper paperwork came through. Raj looked over the paperwork some. His attorney assured him that this was "done all of the time" and would work "with no problem". Raj answered a few questions for the attorney.

A week later, Raj received some forms from his attorney. The letter accompanying the forms explained that the attorney was really representing Raj's employer and that Raj's employer would need to sign them.

Raj took the forms to his employer and explained them as best as he could. His employer read them over and asked:

"Who is this attorney? I didn't hire anyone to represent me!"

Next the supervisor observed:

"Raj, this form says that you supervise a biological research department of 10 people and are making an income of $60,000 per year. But, you really are a lab technician with an income of $18,000 per year. Why is it incorrect?"

Raj suggested that he have his attorney call his supervisor. The attorney called and talked very fast:

> "Don't worry about anything. You just sign the form. Even though it says that I am representing you, I am really representing Raj, and he is paying me. We have to prove that the United States has a special need to have Raj stay here. You just need to offer him this position and salary, then he will refuse it, everything will then be all set. Remember, if Raj does not get this passed, he will be deported."

The Attorney Says it is O.K.

Ethics questions are particularly sticky when a person who is in a position that seems to be "all knowing" says something which seems wrong. Do you stand up to them, or fall back and trust that they must know what they are doing?

Here, the supervisor has the added difficulty of knowing that Raj will surely be deported if the forms are not filed. Not only will he lose a good technician, he will feel guilty about sending a person back to a country that he wants to leave.

More About Raj

Raj's supervisor refused to sign the forms. Raj was so upset about the situation that he took a leave from work. After two months, Raj began to be concerned that he would be deported because he was not working. He called his

supervisor:
> "I have to be able to show that I have been working full-time. Could you please make up some pay stubs for me for the past two months? You don't have to actually pay me, you just would need to make up the check stubs."

By this time, Raj's supervisor had decided not to lie or falsify documents for any reason, even if Raj would be deported. He explained this to Raj and ended with a statement which he had been using a lot lately:

"Raj, I will not go to jail for you."

Draw the Line in Advance

It is very helpful to think about where you stand on issues of this type, before you are asked about them. Here are some questions to consider to help you determine your ethical stance:

- Will your employee's safety be more or less important than reaching corporate goals?

- Will it be more important to keep your staff happy, or to reach your production goals?

- Are you willing to do something illegal in order to reach your goals?

- Are you willing to do something illegal in order to keep your staff happy?

- Are you willing to work with an employee who appears to have a problem with controlled substances?

- Are you willing to keep employing someone who has been convicted of a felony?

Now Stick by Your Beliefs

Once you figure out where you stand on these sticky issues, all you have to do is keep consistent. If you do this, your employees will begin to see the pattern which your decisions follow, and they will actually have to ask you for things less frequently. Carl in the story will not ask his supervisor to lie on a mortgage form again, if his supervisor refuses to do it the first time.

Unfortunately, the requests to do things which are a "little shady" continue forever, so decide what you will and will not do and then stick by your decisions.

SUMMARY OF BOOK ONE

- No one is trained to be a supervisor, supervision is thrust upon you.

- Everyone makes the same first mistakes.

- Most of the time, it's you who are the problem, not the employees ("look to yourself").

- The sensitive supervisor is afraid to confront anyone.

- The belligerent supervisor wants to yell first and ask questions later.

- The regal supervisor is afraid of losing their job.

- The supervisor's personality can be, and must be, tamed.

- If something is going wrong, evaluate the problem by asking "Is this working."

- A supervisor needs to display no emotions, "like a Victorian".

- A supervisor must develop goals both for their work and for their employees.

- A supervisor must decide their ethics, then "draw the line" and stick by it.

A Story About Another Day

Ruth work up a little irritated. She was 44 years old and had nearly finished her first book. She had hired a new employee a month ago, and no matter what she or her supervisory staff tried, the employee was unhappy. The employee would not take responsibility and always blamed others when something went wrong.

At the breakfast table, Ruth outlined a very nice "learn-to-take-responsibility" speech. She went over it with her family, who pronounced it "OK." Later in the morning, she went to look for the employee. To her surprise, in the main office, in front of several other staff members, the employee proclaimed their resignation. Ruth was not surprised about the resignation, just about the "staging" of it. She was actually pretty pleased that this problem was resolved.

Ruth decided that an analysis of what when wrong with this employee would work well in her next supervisor training class.

It was Friday, another week of supervising was done, and more lessons were learned. Ruth began to think about the pizza which was planned for dinner.

INDEX

S

Story About cont'd
    Too Many Decisions, 49
    Wrong Way (belligerent), 27

W

Worried, 12,18,47

Y

Yelling, 11,17,31,37